Photographic Memory:

10 Steps to remember Anything Superfast! Accelerated Learning for Unlimited Memory Efficiency. Create Habits to Help You Improve Your Memory, Focus and Clarity. Mind Hacking!

Table of Contents

Introduction...................7

Chapter 1: What is Photographic Memory? 10

Chapter 2: Eating for Better Memory...................20

Chapter 3: Exercise Your Way to Improved Recall...................32

Chapter 4: Catch Some Zzzzzzz's! 37

Chapter 5: Memorable Meditation...................44

Chapter 6: The Art and Science of Being Mindful...................55

Chapter 7: A Busy Mind Remembers More! 68

Chapter 8: Time for Some Creative Thinking...................78

Chapter 9: The Power of Emotional Recall...................94

Chapter 10: Small Tips and Tricks for Training Your Memory...................110

Chapter 11: Becoming a Memory Champion...................111

Conclusion...................141

© Copyright 2018 by Luke Caldwell - All rights reserved.

The follow eBook is reproduced below with the goal of providing information that is as accurate and reliable as possible. Regardless, purchasing this eBook can be seen as consent to the fact that both the publisher and the author of this book are in no way experts on the topics discussed within and that any recommendations or suggestions that are made herein are for entertainment purposes only. Professionals should be consulted as needed prior to undertaking any of the action endorsed herein.

This declaration is deemed fair and valid by both the American Bar Association and the Committee of Publishers Association and is legally binding throughout the United States.

Furthermore, the transmission, duplication or reproduction of any of the following work including specific information will be considered an illegal act irrespective of if it is done electronically or in print. This extends to creating a secondary or tertiary copy of the work or a recorded copy and is only allowed with express written consent from the Publisher. All additional right reserved.

The information in the following pages is broadly considered to be a truthful and accurate account of facts and as such any inattention, use or misuse of the information in question by the reader will render any resulting actions solely under their purview. There are no scenarios in which the publisher or the original author of this work can be in any fashion deemed liable for any hardship or damages that may befall them after undertaking information described herein.

Additionally, the information in the following pages is intended only for informational purposes and should thus be thought of as universal. As befitting its nature, it is presented without assurance regarding its prolonged validity or interim quality.

Trademarks that are mentioned are done without written consent and can in no way be considered an endorsement from the trademark holder.

Introduction

Congratulations on downloading *Photographic Memory: 10 Steps to Remember Anything Superfast,* and thank you for doing so. If you are interested in supercharging your memorization abilities, you have come to the right place!

There is a lot of conflicting and downright confusing information out there about how memory works, whether or not a photographic memory is possible, and how to train your brain to reach peak memory performance. This handy guide consolidates and explains every step that is necessary to train your memory to maximum efficiency. You will start by learning a bit about how the memory works and what it means to have a photographic memory. Next, we will dive into the steps towards optimizing your recall abilities.

Quite a bit of maximizing your memory potential depends on reaching optimum brain health, so we will teach you how to eat, exercise and sleep for a healthy brain. Next, you will learn about the critical links between mindfulness, meditation, and memory and we will outline how you can learn to meditate effectively and achieve a state of waking mindfulness throughout each day. You will also learn about the critical links between creativity and memory, and how to harness your creativity to improve your memory skills. Additionally, you will discover that you have the ability to transform your emotional habits to further improve your memory.

The last two chapters of this guide cover tips and techniques for learning information, whether it is small amounts or overwhelming lists of information. You will learn enough to train yourself to memorize with the best of them and reach the levels of competitive memorization if you wish. Believe it or not, with the techniques in this book you can learn to memorize a randomly shuffled full deck of cards or even a set of dominos in random order.

There are plenty of books on this subject on the market, so thanks again for choosing this one! Every effort was made to ensure it is full of as much useful information as possible. Please enjoy!

Chapter 1: What is Photographic Memory?

Photographic memory is the supposed ability to take a mental snapshot and be able to recall it in perfect detail in the future. Unfortunately for many readers, this book begins with a massive disappointment. Brace yourself...are you ready? Here it is: *photographic memory is a myth!*

Yes, we are telling you the truth. Although the idea of having a photographic memory is quite popular, often perpetuated by exaggerated stories of spies, famous leaders or ordinary people who could supposedly store mental snapshots and recall them later in perfect detail, there is no recorded proof of anyone with a memory like this. In each case of a person claiming to have a "photographic memory," there has always turned out to be some other explanation for the person's apparent perfect recall. There is one possible exception. In the 1970s, one woman demonstrated an impressive ability that is closer to photographic memory than any recorded ability before or since. The researcher tested her by first showing her a partial image while she had one eye closed. A couple of days later, she would look at the other part of that image with the other eye. She was able to retain the mental picture of the first image and combine the two partial images in her brain so that she could tell the researcher what the whole image looked like.

However, that woman's abilities were never fully tested or confirmed. She ended up marrying the researcher who studied her. After the marriage, she was never the subject of memory testing again. Not enough data on her abilities exists to conclusively prove her memory abilities, and no study participants were able to reproduce her supposed abilities when another researcher decided to investigate the claims made by this woman's researcher husband. As a result, the claim of having a "photographic memory" remains unreliable to this day.

Eidetic Memory

Photographic memory is sometimes confused with an eidetic memory, which is real but very rare. Eidetic memory is a phenomenon in which a vivid "afterimage" of something remains in the mind for up to a few minutes after the original image was seen. This phenomenon gives the person extremely accurate recall abilities, but this recall is never perfect. Eidetic memory exists in 2 to 15 percent of children and very few adults. There are existing claims that you can train yourself to have an eidetic memory, but these are false;

an eidetic memory is a quality that you either have or do not have.

But There is Still Great News!

Now that you are feeling disappointed and discouraged about your non-existent potential to achieve photographic or eidetic memory, you are probably asking yourself why you bothered to look at this book. Do not fear, because there is still much that can be learned!

Now that we have disappointed you, the good news is that the term "photographic memory" is still immensely popular and a widely accepted term for having the ability to recall experiences with great detail and clarity. So as far as the general population is concerned, this book is about training your brain to have a photographic memory. If you read the instructions, follow the suggestions and practice the memory training techniques, you will be able to truthfully claim that you have a photographic memory, at least as far as the way that most people in society define that term. Only you (and a few others) know the truth!

Although you may not ever be able to recall an event or scene with such perfect clarity that you remember every single detail, you still have the potential to improve your memory to an astonishing degree! After practicing the methods in this book, many people have been able to quickly memorize the order of a randomly shuffled deck of cards or an entire set of dominoes placed in random order. Other than these party tricks, you can also train your brain to retain critical information, such as quickly recalling faces and names, remembering long lists of information without having it written down, or easily reciting the directions to a location after only hearing it one time. So, have hope – although you may never achieve the mythical "photographic memory," if you follow the instructions in this book for training your brain, you can make many people *think* you have a photographic memory!

How Does Memory Work?

Before we get into training your brain, let's take a look at how the memory process works so you have a clearer understanding of what you are trying to master.

When we talk about **memory**, we are talking about the process by which the brain acquires, stores, retains and later retrieves information. There are three major processes in memory: **encoding, storage,** and **retrieval**.

When we experience an event, person, place or thing, the details of that experience are translated through our perception, the involvement of our five senses in the experience. This is the beginning of the **encoding** process. Details about sight, sounds, touch, smell, and taste are all transmitted to the hippocampus, which is a part of the brain that puts all of the details together into a single experience. Scientists believe that the hippocampus and another part of the brain called the frontal cortex to analyze experiences and "decide" if they're worth storing for long-term memory.

Once your senses have perceived an experience, chemical and electric messages fire between nerve cells, forming a specific pathway within the brain. This specific pathway is related to that experience, and the more times you encounter that experience, the stronger that pathway becomes.

An experience can only be properly encoded if you are paying attention; thankfully, the brain filters out most of what we encounter on a daily basis. Without this filter, our memories would be full within the first hour of a day!

After encoding comes the **storage** process of the memory. A sensation is first stored in **short-term memory**, which can typically only hold approximately 7 items at a time for about 30 seconds. If the information is important, it will be repeated and used often, which leads to it being stored in **long-term memory**. After the information has moved to this part of the memory, it is called "**retained**" memory. Your long-term memory has an amazing capacity. So far, there seems to be no limit to the amount of information it can store or the length of time that it can store it.

When we want to remember something, our brain goes through the **retrieval** process, which brings the information back from our unconscious mind to our conscious mind. When we have trouble remembering something, it is often because it was not properly encoded or stored in the first place. This happens often when we are distracted. This distraction could be due to stress, excessive strong emotions, or too much going on around you. Or if you are having trouble remembering something that you studied, it may be because you studied in an environment that was not conducive to studying or because you did not repeat the information to yourself often enough. In other words, you are responsible for making sure that important information is properly encoded and stored so that you can recall it when you need to.

Many people think of themselves as having "good" or "bad" memories, but the truth is that most people have the same potential for memory ability, assuming there are no underlying conditions damaging brain function. Since almost all of us have the potential to achieve phenomenal recall abilities, that means that the techniques in this book could turn you from someone who has a "bad" or average memory to someone who remembers great quantities of information with seemingly minimal effort!

Chapter 2: Eating for Better Memory

Since our nutrition – or lack thereof – has a huge impact on our physical and emotional

fitness, it only makes sense that healthy eating can be hugely beneficial to our ability to recall facts and experiences. This chapter will cover the various nutrients that you should incorporate into your diet for better brain health and improved memory, as well as the foods that you should avoid if you're hoping to improve your recall skills.

1. **Omega-3's**: Lately it seems that you cannot get through a day without hearing another expert touting the benefits of omega-3's, and the memory experts are no exception! These oils are found in fatty fish, like salmon, halibut, and tuna, and they play an important role in brain function. A 2016 study released by Harvard Medical School shows that these powerful – albeit smelly – oils can reverse the decline of memory, too. If you do not like eating the types of fish rich in this type of oil, consider taking a fish oil supplement that includes plenty of Omega-3's.

If you do invest in an Omega-3 supplement, just make sure that it is a supplement that has been verified by the United States Pharmacopeia, or USP. This verification means that it has been analyzed and tests have confirmed that it contains the ingredients that are printed on the label, and that the potency of the nutrients is accurate. It also means that there are no harmful substances that were accidentally included and that the desirable nutrients will absorb into your body when you take the supplement. Look for a little "USP Verified" mark on any supplements that you purchase!

2. **Fruits and Vegetables**: Omega-3 oils are known to reduce inflammation, but what about other anti-inflammatory foods? In general, foods that are high in antioxidants help lower inflammation in the body. You can find high levels of antioxidants in many fruits and vegetables. As it turns out, these foods have a significant impact on your mental health, too. People who eat a wide variety of vegetables and fruits are at

decreased risks of developing dementia or any other age-related type of mental decline than people who eat less healthy foods. This has been proven by multiple studies over decades of research.

3. **Caffeine:** Coffee-lovers, rejoice! Recent research from the Radiological Society of North America has shown that drinking just 2 cups of coffee per day can help boost short-term memory function. Additional research has also shown that *when* you consume caffeine makes a difference, too. One study shows that taking a supplement containing caffeine was beneficial to students' memories if they took it right after learning some new information. The benefits from the caffeine were shown to last for up to 24 hours.

4. **Vitamin D:** This nutrient is essential to many functions of the body, including memory. More than one study in recent years has linked low levels of vitamin D with quicker memory loss and greater risks of dementia than those who have healthy levels of vitamin D. Many people are at risk of being deficient of vitamin D, especially those of us who live in cold climates. Supplements for this vitamin are widely available, but you should ask your doctor to test your vitamin D levels before taking a supplement. Again, make sure to look for a "USP Verified" stamp of approval on your vitamin bottle.

5. **Cocoa:** Like fruits and vegetables, cocoa is rich in antioxidants. These particular antioxidants are called flavonoids, and they are quite helpful to the brain because they encourage brain

cells and blood vessels in the brain to grow. They also cause more blood to flow to the brain segments that take part in memory encoding and storage. More blood flow means more oxygen and nutrients are going to these areas, so it is great for your memory! Flavonoids are most dense in dark chocolate and non-existent in white chocolate, so the most memory benefits can be derived from eating chocolate with 70% cacao or higher. Incidentally, the consumption of dark chocolate has also been associated with a higher visual function. Eating just a little of high-quality dark chocolate each day has many proven benefits to your health, so this added bonus of improved memory should have us all jumping for a (small) chocolate bar!

6. **Protein:** Along with benefits to muscle and endurance, protein has also been

proven to improve memory. One study showed that eating a protein-heavy breakfast enhanced the accuracy of short-term memory, possibly because eating more protein leads to more stable glucose levels in the blood. Consider adding some lean sources of protein to your breakfast, like eggs and turkey bacon, to improve your short-term memory abilities.

7. **Choline:** Here's another great reason to eat eggs! A nutrient called choline can instantly boost short-term memory, and just one little egg yolk contains 115 mg of choline. The benefit of this nutrient to short-term memory has been shown in several studies. There are many ways to incorporate eggs into your diet, so get creative and eat your eggs!

8. **Luteolin:** This nutrient, found in celery and peppers, fights the type of brain inflammation that can come with aging. With the reduction of brain inflammation comes a reduced risk of age-related memory problems. The takeaway is to eat sources of this nutrient if you want to stay sharp as you age! It is okay if you do not enjoy raw peppers or celery. These vegetables can be cooked and added to a variety of delicious recipes, including soups, stews, and stir-fry dinners.

9. **Less Added Sugar and Refined Carbs:** Eating foods with a lot of added sugar, such as that found in sodas and candy, has been linked with poor short-term memory. Additionally, people who ate foods with high added sugar have reduced brain volumes and overall poorer memory abilities. If you do enjoy

sweetened beverages and food, try plain beverages (like iced tea) or unsweetened cereal and just adding a little sugar or honey. This will cut your sugar intake immensely since pre-sweetened foods typically have much more sugar than you are likely to add on your own.

Highly refined carbohydrates, like those found in cereals, white rice, cookies, and white bread can also be dangerous. These processed carbs cause the sugar levels in your blood to suddenly and rapidly increase as they are digested. Large fluctuations in blood sugar levels are dangerous for many parts of your body, and one result can be reduced functioning of the brain. On top of that, a study of children showed that those who ate more refined carbs had poorer short-term and working memories. The foods they ate included french fries and noodles. Instead of consuming these highly refined carbohydrates, try incorporating whole grains and complex carbs such as sweet potatoes into your diet.

10. **Less Alcohol:** Alcohol is worth cutting back on, too. While occasional controlled drinking is not harmful, researchers have found proof that binge drinking (quickly consuming enough alcohol to raise the blood alcohol levels above the legal limit) causes difficulties in memory recall and can damage the hippocampus. If you will recall from Chapter 1, the hippocampus is important in the brain's memory storage process. If you find yourself at a party or other situation where you might normally binge drink, try limiting yourself to one drink per hour and drink a glass of water in between alcoholic

beverages. If you find you are unable to stop or control your drinking, there are many options for getting help. Your future memory ability depends on it!

11. **Red Wine:** Although binge drinking is clearly unhealthy for many reasons, research has shown that a glass or two of red wine can be beneficial. Red wine contains a compound called *resveratrol*, which acts as an antioxidant and has many health benefits, including the slowing and possible reversal of age-related memory loss. If you're not into red wine, have no fear. The compound is also found in red grapes, some berries, and peanuts. There are also some supplements available, but ask a health expert before taking one.

If your head is spinning just a little from all this nutritional advice, here's a quick summary: Eat fish with Omega-3's or find a good supplement for this nutrient. Eat a lot of different fruits and vegetables and include a moderate amount of caffeine in your diet. Ask your doctor to test your vitamin D levels and take a supplement if needed. Eat a small amount of dark chocolate and drink one or two glasses of red wine every now and then. Eat plenty of lean protein, including eggs, and incorporate celery and peppers into your diet. Limit the number of sugary foods and drinks you consume, and avoid refined carbs. Try to avoid binge drinking altogether.

There are plenty of delicious ways to incorporate all these suggestions into your diet, so enjoy! Keep reading to find the next step to a superb memory.

Chapter 3: Exercise Your Way to Improved Recall

Now that you know how to eat for maximum recall ability, let's talk about exercise. It is not

everyone's favorite topic, but it is a necessity nonetheless. You have heard the myriad of benefits to exercising from your doctor, magazines, news shows, and well-intentioned family members. Well, as it turns out, an exceptional memory is one more potential benefit of working out.

How Exercise Helps Memory

There are a ton of in-depth scientific studies that prove the positive link between exercise and improved memory, but the bottom line is that exercise increases your rate of circulation. An increased rate of circulation means that more oxygen is going to your brain, so it can function more efficiently. Specifically, researchers have found that exercising 4 hours or less after learning something new can help you to retain that information much better than if you had been inactive for a long time after learning. The reason for this seems to be that exercise causes a better flow of blood, leading to increased activity in the hippocampus of the brain.

On top of this benefit, exercise has been shown by multiple studies to improve overall brain function, including memory. One particular study showed that not only does exercise help prevent age-related memory loss, but it can *improve* your ability to retain and recall information! The results of this study showed that aerobic exercise (e.g., walking or running) and anaerobic exercise (e.g., weight lifting) each affected different types of memory, but the important result was that they both improved memory abilities. For the best overall improvement to your memory, then, the recommendation is to try and incorporate both aerobic and resistant types of exercise into your routine.

The Dangers of Not Working Out

Just in case you are still sitting on the couch and thinking that perhaps you can do without this part of your memory upgrade, you should also know that staying *inactive* can be very harmful to your brain function. One study on rats showed that a sedentary lifestyle causes the neurons (nerve cells) in the brains to have extra branches. At first, this sounds like a good thing, but it turns out that the extra branches are related to regulation of involuntary functions of the body, like breathing. The extra branches cause the nervous system to be overstimulated. This overstimulation can cause problems like damage to the heart or lungs and a dangerous increase to your blood pressure. Since leading an inactive lifestyle can have such a detrimental effect on the shape of your brain's nerve cells, just think about what the dangers to the rest of your brain's functions, like memory, might be!

If you're a true-blue couch potato and you feel like you might be allergic to exercise, you can try adding just little bits of exercise at a time.

Even a brisk twenty-minute walk has been proven to increase activity in the brain. Twenty minutes is just a minuscule portion of your day when you think about it, and the benefits will far outweigh the risk of missing your couch for that amount of time! Go ahead and give it a try – we sincerely doubt that you'll be sorry.

Chapter 4: Catch Some Zzzzzzz's!

While we're on the topic of better health habits, we should talk about the one that is seriously lacking for most adults lately: sleep. Although caffeine in moderate amounts can benefit your memory, it is no substitute for a great night of sleep.

Sleep and Memory Consolidation

When we sleep, our brain goes through much of the process of *memory consolidation*, which is when recently learned experiences are sorted and the important ones are changed into long-term memories. Various structural and chemical changes in the nervous system cause this conversion, and much of this depends on us getting enough sleep. Some memory consolidation can happen when we are awake, but the most important parts happen when we are asleep.

Even if you can't get a full night of sleep, your memory abilities can benefit from a short nap! One study had two groups of adults memorize illustrated cards. One group took a forty-minute nap after memorizing, and the other group stayed awake for forty minutes. Then both groups were tested on how much they remembered from what they had previously memorized. To the surprise of the researchers, the group that took a nap showed significantly better recall abilities.

A similar study was performed on two groups of children who were in the age group of 10 to 14. Some of the children were given memory training, then they were tested on the same day. They did not sleep between the training and testing. The rest of the children were given memory training in the evening, allowed to sleep for a full night, and then tested in the morning. The results were that the group that was allowed to sleep before testing performed significantly better.

What Happens When We Don't Get Enough Sleep?

Since sleep is critical to proper memory storage, it follows that sleep deprivation causes problems in our ability to form new memories. It only takes a single night of sleep deprivation to significantly reduce our ability to retain any new information! This discovery is somewhat concerning, considering how sleep-deprived most adults are these days.

Not only does sleep deprivation hinder your ability to commit new information to memory, but it also negatively impacts your *working memory*, which is the brain's system for temporarily holding information available for processing while you perform complex tasks. In other words, it's your ability to work with information as it is given to you. It can also be called your short-term memory. It is critical to your ability to reason, make decisions and behave rationally.

When you are sleep deprived, your brain's functions are noticeably sluggish and it goes into a kind of "conservation mode," shutting down some of the more basic functions. Your working memory then steps in to make up for some of these basic functions to help us perform complex tasks. However, this system of compensation is not perfect. Research has shown that in this state, people are much more easily distracted and more likely to overreact to emotional stimuli. As a result, the working memory is compromised and we are less able to act rationally.

How Do We Get More Sleep?
People are busier than ever lately, and it can be easy to sacrifice sleep to pack more activity and productivity in your day. But by now you should be able to see how critical sleep is to your goals of achieving superb memory

abilities. If you wish to one day wow your friends and family with your remarkable memory or be able to memorize great quantities of information for work or school, you must make sleep a priority!

Experts recommend that adults of all ages get seven to nine hours of sleep per night. For you to achieve this, we suggest following these helpful hints:

- *Make a schedule* for sleep. Schedule your lights-out and wake-up times, and stick to them just as rigidly as you would a business meeting. Even on the weekend, when it's tempting to stay up late and sleep in, you need to stay committed to the same bedtimes and wake-up times.

- *Turn off the TV, computer and all mobile devices* an hour before your lights-out time. We have all heard of the studies that show how disruptive those bright, shiny screens are for our sleep. If we are looking at them too close to bedtime, the quality of our sleep can be significantly decreased.

- *Unplug or cover anything in your bedroom with standby lights.* Those little round red, blue, or green lights can be equally disruptive to the quality of your sleep, even if they seem small and insignificant. You may fall asleep with them in the room just fine, but just the presence of those lights can interfere with your brain waves while you sleep, and as a result, you do not sleep as restfully or as deeply.

- *Avoid alcohol and coffee after dinner.* It may seem that alcohol helps you sleep, but in all actuality, it keeps you from reaching the deep sleep that your memory needs. Caffeine may keep you awake or cause poor sleep quality, too.

If you follow these tips and make a sincere effort make sleep a high priority, we are confident that you will be reaping the memory benefits in as little as a few days.

Chapter 5: Memorable Meditation

When you picture someone who meditates regularly, you may picture a serenely calm person who is rational, grounded and in touch with their feelings. Or, if you have a less favorable opinion of meditation, you may form an entirely different picture in your head. But what you may not picture is someone who has a remarkable memory. The mental benefits of meditation have been studied and widely publicized for decades now, but many people may not be aware that memory is among them.

What is Meditation?
Meditation by definition is simply the practice of using various techniques to train attention and awareness, thereby achieving an emotionally calm and mentally clear state of being. There are a large variety of techniques that fall under the umbrella of meditation,

including visualization, chanting, breathing techniques, various physical poses, guided practices, and focusing on particular objects, both real and imagined.

People who meditate may do so because they want to reduce stress, feel less physical or emotional pain, increase their inner peace or improve their breath control. You may have heard of many of its many benefits, including anxiety reduction, improved emotional health, lowered blood pressure, enhanced self-awareness and improved concentration. Some people find that they are able to sleep better once they have practiced meditation for a while, and others use it as part of their addiction recovery program. Most people who practice meditation find that they have a better overall feeling of well-being and compassion towards themselves and others. What many people may not realize is that by practicing meditation, they improve their overall brain function, including their memory.

How Does Meditation Improve Memory?
Essentially, meditation is an exercise that slows down your mind's processing. By practicing meditation, you train your mind and give yourself more control of your thoughts. Ultimately, this control can also greatly improve your memory.

You may recall that *working memory* is essentially the short-term memory, where new information is held temporarily to help you perform complex tasks. After these tasks, information that is useful may be committed to long-term memory. We use our working memory multiple times per day, whether it is helping us get to a new address or retaining the names of new business associates in a meeting. As it turns out, the working memory can be strengthened by meditation.

During a meditation practice, we pay attention to our thoughts; specifically, we either try to focus on one thought, process or object, or we simply sit and observe our thoughts without trying to control or react to them. Either way, we are much more focused than normal.

Through modern technology that allows brain scans, researchers have been able to get a good look at what happens in the brain before and after meditation practices. These brain scans have shown that meditation causes our brains to stop processing information as actively as they normally would. This sounds like it might be a bad thing, but it means that there is significantly more focus in a brain that has been trained by meditation. More focus means less anxiety, less distraction, and a much better ability to commit information to memory!

Researchers believe that the reason for this increased focus from meditation is that people gain better control over their *alpha waves*, which form a kind of screen for everyday distractions. When you are better able to block out distractions, you can process more important information better, thus increasing your chances of recalling it later. This ability has been shown to improve in as few as eight weeks of regular meditation, even in people who had never attempted meditation before.

Not only does meditation improve your ability to focus, but it also has been proven to cause an increase in the amount of the gray matter (which contains neuron cells) in your brain. This gray matter generally decreases with age, leading to decreased brain function and memory abilities. But thanks to its positive effects on gray matter and alpha-wave control, meditation can benefit memory abilities for people from all generations, including the elderly. Research has shown astonishing possibilities for the benefits of meditation to memory, notably the ability to help prevent Alzheimer's disease and dementia.

How to Incorporate Meditation into Your Life

Now that you know how great meditation can be for your capacity to remember, you're probably wondering how to get started. If you are a beginner to meditation, it's best to start small and build from there. Follow these tips to begin your very own meditation practice:

1. **Find a regular time during the day** that is most conducive for you to meditate. This could be at the beginning of the day, lunchtime, right after work, or right before bed. The key is to find a time when distractions are minimal and you are best able to focus your mind.

2. Schedule just **5 minutes each day** and build from there. **Set a timer** when you start, so you don't need to keep glancing at the clock during your practice. At first, 5 minutes may seem far too long, but eventually, you'll get used to it and

at that point, you may want to try for 10 minutes each day. But don't rush your progress.

3. **Find a comfortable place to sit**. You can sit in a chair with your feet down on the floor. If you would prefer, you can sit on the floor instead. If you need it, feel free to use a pillow or cushion for support. If you would like to try lying down, go ahead and do so, but some people do not recommend this.

4. Eventually, you may want to **create a meditation space** in your home, but this is not necessary when you're first starting out. Keep this in mind for the future.

5. An easy beginning meditation practice is to **count your breath**. Try counting each inhales and exhales with the same number, like this (thinking, not speaking aloud): "One" (inhale), "One" (exhale), "Two" (inhale), "Two" (exhale), and so on. Once you hit Ten, start over. Or you can just think to yourself, "In, out, in, out…"

6. **When your mind wanders** (which is normal and ok!), notice your distraction and then start paying attention to your breath again. Start counting again from the beginning if you do not remember where you left off. **Do not be upset with yourself** because you let your mind wander! But do pat yourself on the back for the times that you notice that your attention has strayed because taking that notice means that you are becoming more aware of your thoughts.

7. Try **noticing sensations in your body** while you breathe, once you get used to the counting. Where do you notice the inhalations? And the exhalations? Do you feel any tightness or discomfort anywhere? If so, try focusing your breath energy on those

areas and notice how the tightness gradually loosens up.

8. **When distracting thoughts arise**, try to just notice them without engaging them. Don't dive into them and try to solve them. Just acknowledge them and move on.

9. **Do this every day** to make it a habit. After many weeks (possibly months, if you're a tough sell), it will become as habitual as making your bed or brushing your teeth.

10. **If you feel like nothing is changing** as a result of your meditation practice, be patient. Meditation is not about finding profound insights or suddenly becoming serene and wise. It is about accepting your thoughts and

surroundings without judgment in each passing moment. You are probably changing gradually without even realizing it, gaining attributes like greater concentration, self-control, and the memory capacity that we are seeking.

If you are interested in delving further into meditation, enhancing your practice or just learning more, there are plenty of resources out there. YouTube offers many guided meditation channels, your Google Play or iTunes stores have meditation apps, the internet offers blogs and forums aplenty, and your local library has books and videos that can guide you. The important part is to keep learning and practicing. The ultimate goal of this book is to improve your memory ability, but you may reap a myriad of benefits by pursuing an interest in meditation!

Chapter 6: The Art and Science of Being Mindful

Right now, you may be thinking that there is no need to cover mindfulness. *"Didn't we just cover that in the meditation chapter??!"* Well, yes and no. While it is true that meditation helps you achieve a state of mindfulness, the two concepts are not necessarily intrinsically linked.

What is Mindfulness?

Mindfulness refers to the state of being aware of your thoughts, feelings, and surroundings at any given moment, whether or not you are meditating. "Being present" is a description often given to people when they are mindful. Meditation can be the formal practice of mindfulness, but mindfulness by itself is something that you can practice in any situation.

In general, people have a bad habit of focusing on the negative and overlooking the positive parts of life. We can be so ruled by regrets from the past or anxieties of the future that we are unaware of our present situation. We are also quick to label thoughts, feelings, and circumstances as "good" or "bad." In contrast, when we are mindful, we carefully observe our thoughts and feelings without labeling or judging them.

Mindfulness can be a healthy way to become aware of emotions that you hide under the surface. Without you being aware of them, these hidden emotions can be causing problems in relationships or distracting you from focusing on your current situation. Mindfulness means simply living in each moment instead of focusing on the past or present.

There are a great number of benefits to practicing mindfulness in your daily life, including improved relationships, decreased depression and anxiety, lowered stress levels and improved overall health. Additionally, mindfulness training can improve your concentration and memory.

Mindfulness and Memory

Similar to meditation practice, mindfulness training helps you filter out distracting and potentially damaging thoughts so that you can focus on information as it is given to you. This increased focus leads to better information storage and consequently better recall of what you have learned and experienced.

A 2016 study of almost 300 students in the field of psychology showed that mindfulness training can improve your ability to recall objects through your recognition-memory, which is what you use to recognize people or things that you have seen before. On top of this, mindfulness training has also been shown to reduce the risk of decline in brain function associated with aging.

How to Bring More Mindfulness to Each Day

A great beginning to mindfulness is the meditation practice we discussed in chapter 5. However, there are many more ways to begin practicing mindfulness in your daily life. Try each of the following suggestions and take note of which ones seem the most effective for you:

- **Mindful listening:** When listening to another person, many of us have the bad habit of letting our minds wander and not being fully present. We think about the other person, but not always what they are saying. Or we are completely distracted by our own thoughts or surroundings while only pretending to listen! The next time you are listening to someone, whether they are someone you love or not, try using this time to exercise mindfulness. Focus all your attention on that person and what they are saying, even if it seems mundane and unimportant. They will truly appreciate the attention and may decide to reciprocate and give you more attention the next time you speak.

- **Household chores:** Since most of us spend a good deal of time doing household chores, these are excellent opportunities to practice mindfulness. The next time you have to fold laundry, wash dishes or make dinner, try focusing your entire attention to that particular task, and continue to focus on it as each moment. Notice the aromas of the food you cook and watch the transformation the raw ingredients go through as you combine and heat them to make a dish. Pay attention to the textures of the clothes you fold, the sounds that the dishes make as they bump into each other in the soapy water, and the light and temperature of the room you're in. As you practice this mindfulness, you'll begin to feel that each little act is a special ritual. You will be in tune with your world and able to transform ordinary chores into harmonious parts of your day.

- **Mindful Eating:** Since most of us have lives that are jam-packed with activities, we often eat meals on the run, while making phone calls or driving to the next practice or event. Fast food is a staple in our diet, and many families rarely sit down to eat dinner together – and when they do, it's often in front of the television. Try bringing mindfulness to one meal per day to start off. Sit down in a designated eating space with no distractions. Leave the cell phone in another room and turn off the TV. Take time to savor each bite, noticing the texture, flavor, and aroma of your food. Take small bites and eat slowly, and pay attention to how your body feels as you nourish it. Notice when you feel full and make a point of ending the meal right then. This practice is not only good for your brain, but it has the added benefit of aiding healthy digestion and weight loss. Soon you'll find that you want to practice mindfulness every time you eat, and those fast food meals will be a thing of the past!

- **No More Multi-tasking!** Lately, the ability to "multi-task" has been considered a virtue, something that we like to brag about when talking to friends, family or potential employers. But the truth is that multi-tasking is the opposite of productive; it spreads out attention too thin and makes us more liable to make mistakes. Instead of trying to do multiple things at a time, focus on one task at a time. Pay attention to phone conversations, answer emails while focusing solely on the computer screen and keep your attention on the present discussion in meetings instead of surreptitiously checking the messages on your phone. You will be amazed at how much more you are able to remember from each part of your day and the improved quality and efficiency of your work.

- **Stop Rushing:** All too often, we try to get things done as quickly as possible so that we can move on to the next thing. We focus on deadlines, productivity and the number of tasks that we can pack into a day instead of appreciating each moment as it comes. Try slowing your pace down physically for a change and see what happens. When you go grocery shopping, pay attention to each item as you check it off your list. Drive and walk at reasonable speeds instead of rushing to shave minutes off your commute. Take the time to connect with a client instead of being focused on a quick sale. You'll find that you take away value from each experience when the goal is to be present instead of moving as quickly as possible.

- **Mindful Movement:** Whether you are exercising or just walking between offices at work, pay attention to the sensations in your body. Appreciate the movements of each limb and the feelings of your feet as they hit the ground beneath you. Notice how your clothes feel as they move against your skin. Take note of all of the little characteristics of the scene around you, whether you are indoors or outdoors. This mindfulness is a practice you can incorporate into your day without taking any extra time in your busy schedule. You may find that you appreciate your body and ability to move much more if you are mindful of each individual movement.

- **Take some time to do "nothing.":** Our culture applauds productivity and frowns on idleness, so most of us have lost the ability to sit still and do nothing at all. In fact, we tend to feel guilty if we even consider spending time doing "nothing." But the fact of the matter is that we really do not need to be focused on a task at every moment of the day! Try taking a little bit of "nothing" time each day, even if you are only able to do so for just a few minutes. Set a timer if you need to, then sit silently in your favorite chair or couch. Sit outside in the sun if the weather is pleasant, or go to a favorite park and enjoy a gentle breeze. You might be surprised at how much pleasure you derive from just a few minutes of just "being" while doing nothing at all.

- **Notice Your Senses:** Another mindfulness practice is to notice your five senses in any given moment. Pay attention to smells as you go about your day. Listen to quiet noises outside your window or even in the same room: the hum of your computer, the washing machine in the other room, or the murmured voices of a quiet conversation down the hall. Notice the breeze on your skin, drops of rain on your face or the feel of a favorite shirt on your arms. Take a few moments to appreciate sights that you normally take for granted, like the sky during your evening commute, trees in the parking lot or children playing outside the school when you pick up your child in the afternoon. Notice the taste of your morning coffee as you sip it while catching up on email. Bringing awareness to your senses like this helps you to be engaged in each moment, instead of being preoccupied with distracting thoughts. You may even find that this sensory awareness brings a new sense of amazement to previous moments that seemed commonplace.

Following these suggestions for mindfulness training should help you to be more present in each moment as it passes. Not only will you reap the benefits of reduced stress, lowered anxiety and depression, and heightened sensory awareness, but you will notice that you remember so much more from each day. As you bring mindfulness into each day, your memory abilities will be strengthened because you are paying attention to so many more details that used to pass you by unnoticed.

Chapter 7: A Busy Mind Remembers More!

It seems counterintuitive that, after two chapters describing the benefits of slowing down, paying attention and making time to be still, we should follow with a chapter professing that you need to keep your mind busy! This is one of those cases in which it's best to strike a happy medium. If you want to improve your memory, it is critical to learn the meditation and mindfulness practices previously outlined. However, you do not want to give yourself *too much* downtime, because the memory functions of people who allow themselves too much idle time tend to suffer.

Keep Your Calendar Full

While it is important to allow yourself time to be mindful, exercise and get enough sleep, you should also make sure you are living a full and well-rounded life. Specifically, this means keeping busy with hobbies and a social life. Most people who are in school or work full-time while raising children do not have to worry about this problem. Usually, they have more than enough to do between school fundraisers, study groups, playdates, sports practices and family time. However, people who are not busy with family or a full-time career could benefit from this advice.

Many people over the age of 50, who are retired, single or empty-nesters may want to try making sure they keep enough to do on their calendar. One study surveyed 330 adults ages 50 to 89 on the busyness of their calendar. Participants were asked to rate their day-to-day busyness, and they answered various questions about their schedule so that researchers could gauge how active their lives were. The participants also underwent tests that measured their memory abilities along with information processing speed, vocabulary and reasoning abilities.

The results of this test were that, on average, the adults who kept a busier life had better cognitive function scores than those whose calendars were comparatively empty. One researcher noted that the study did not thoroughly address whether a busy life improved cognitive function or vice versa, but it was speculated that staying busy and active might stimulate the brain, leading to intellectual growth. Specifically, keeping busy gives you more opportunities to meet new people and encounter new situations, which accelerates your brain's learning and growth. Since memory is a huge part of the cognitive function, it should be no surprise that staying busy helps people's memory abilities as well. The study noted that the two types of memory that are benefited from a busy calendar are *working memory* (a.k.a. short-term memory, previously defined in Chapters 4 and 5) and *episodic memory* (memory involved in recalling times and places).

The Dangers of Idleness

Although retirement is something that most Americans take for granted as the inevitable reward for their decades of work, retirement is actually a very recent and – some might argue – unnatural development to our culture. For thousands of years, humans kept working until physically unable to do so, simply because they had to and because that was how things were done. It is only in the past one hundred years or so that many of us have been retiring from work once we reach a certain age. In the 1800s, most men over the age of sixty-five were still working, but now that age is often considered the "golden age" when we can retire to a life of blissful ease.

Unfortunately, it seems that retirement may put your mental skills at high risk of decline. A 2010 study of thousands of retirees in America and Europe discovered that retirement leads to a reduction of thinking along with the long-anticipated reduction of physical labor. If you have ever taken a long vacation from work or school, you have probably experienced this phenomenon to a certain extent. When you return from vacation, you often find that you have to put extra mental effort into tasks that came easily before you left. When you relax, you no longer have the pressure of having to think creatively, find solutions to problems, impress potential clients or meet deadlines. While relaxation itself is not intrinsically a bad thing, this is a case in which too much of a good thing can be damaging.

The study mentioned in the previous paragraph used a test that included remembering lists of words. The researchers administered this cognitive test to the thousands of retirees they studied, and to senior adults who were still working. When they compiled their data, they specifically compared the cognitive skills of workers in their fifties to those of retirees in their sixties. Their finding, among other data, was that the more likely the sixty-somethings were to be retired, the worse their cognitive skills were in comparison to the younger group! Another conclusion drawn from this multi-country study is that the later you retire, the smarter you typically remain. Although many of us in America envy those in certain European countries who are able to retire at younger ages, the reality is that we keep our minds and memories sharper in America by continuing to work later in life.

Another factor of retirement and/or growing older that leads to quieter lives is decreased social interaction. When people your age or older pass away or move to sunnier climes, you may find that you can go entire days without speaking to anyone other than your pet cat. Unfortunately, a shrinking social circle can be as damaging to your brain function as leaving the workforce. When you interact with other people, you are forced to expand your perspective and think creatively. By keeping other people's experiences and opinions in mind, you exercise your working memory. You also constantly learn from the stories and information that they share with you. It follows that the fewer relationships you have, the fewer opportunities you have to engage your working memory. Your world shrinks, and so does the amount of information that you need to recall on a regular basis.

What Does This Mean for You?

As much as you may hate the idea of working into your late sixties or even longer, your memory will remain much sharper if you do so. If physical disadvantages, financial independence or other circumstances lead you to early retirement, make goals to keep yourself busy and social.

However, please do keep in mind everything that you have already learned in the previous chapters of this book. If you keep *too* busy, you most likely don't make time to eat properly, the quality and quantity of your sleep suffer, you probably don't have time to exercise and you certainly aren't making time to meditate or practice mindfulness. Additionally, the stress hormones from being too busy might actually hurt the brain. With all these downsides, being over-busy is definitely not the key to improving your memory abilities!

Instead of staying busy simply for the sake of being busy, find things that are interesting and meaningful to you and fill your calendar with these things. Make social appointments with friends, try new hobbies that seem interesting and pay attention to community events. You can attend local lectures and performances, look into making day trips to nearby destinations, and volunteer for a worthy cause. You can also try getting involved in your church or some other social organization so that you continue to meet new people and form new relationships. There are many engaging activities that can fill your calendar without adding to your stress levels. Believe us, your brain will thank you!

The memory is basically like a muscle. When it is exercised, it stays in shape and even improves. However, if it is not used, it gets weaker and weaker. By staying in touch with other people and being involved in a variety of activities, you give your memory plenty of new information to chew on every single day. So keep "flexing" those memory muscles and keep your calendar full.

Chapter 8: Time for Some Creative Thinking

Whether you think of yourself as a creative person or not, within you lies a spark of creativity. Creativity is simply the use of imagination or original ideas, and we all have the potential to be creative. Even if you've never penned a story or poem, picked up a paintbrush or captured a beautiful picture through a camera lens, you can be a creative individual. Every person on earth has a unique perspective, a different view that frames the world, and this perspective is the frame by which memories are formed.

The Link Between Creativity and Memory

Since your memories are how you store, connect or interpret your experiences, your memories actually reflect your individual creativity. You may remember a certain person that you saw last week because they looked a little like your Aunt Sally, or that bakery across the street might spark memories of your mother's apple pie. A beautiful painting in a shop window might bring back memories of a rainbow you saw as a child. Whatever your memories and intellectual connections might be, they are unique to *you* alone, and they show your potential to be creative.

Not only are memory and creativity intrinsically linked, but you can also boost your memory powers by exercising your creativity. When you strive to be creative, either by coming up with new ideas or making something artistically fresh, you draw on your prior experiences, whether or not you are aware of it.

Many people think that creativity is the exact opposite of memory. After all, the things we remember already exist, while creativity strives to come up with something new and fresh, right? This seems true, but it is not exactly accurate. In truth, creative insights always come from combinations of material that already exists in our minds. There are no new ideas that simply appear out of thin air; you build on existing ideas to come up with new ones.

Your memories are the raw materials for your creativity. As a result, when you exercise your creative abilities, you force your brain to form new pathways between memories. As you become more creative and come up with seemingly "new" concepts, old experiences that once seemed like separate events can become linked in your mind. This process leads to stronger memories as you draw on them again and again.

Some of you may think that you are just "not creative." There is a widespread false conception that creativity is primarily found in the sensory arts. While it is true that creativity is most obvious in painting, dance, music, sculpting, etc., you can find the ability to be creative even in the most logical of activities. Scientists and mathematicians must be creative on a daily basis to come up with new links between data or new formulas to explain old phenomena. Even the most mundane activities can require creativity at times. You think creatively when you face daily problems that require quick solutions, like when you have to housetrain a puppy or clean up the mess from a broken dishwasher.

How to Boost Your Creativity

Since your memory abilities can be improved by exercising your powers of creativity, how exactly

should you go about this process? Lucky for you, we've compiled a list of suggestions for flexing your creative muscles:

- **Cultivate boredom:** We spend so much time focused on finding entertainment that we rarely give our minds the opportunity to wander creatively. When we have downtime, we are quick to reach for the remote control or scroll through our phones in search of something to do. But if you make a point of reducing your entertainment, you give your creativity the opportunity to roam freely. Being "bored" prompts your brain to create something new, whether it is just wandering through ideas or coming up with something to do. To give this a try, go for a week without turning on your TV and see what kinds of ideas you come up with for entertaining yourself.

- **Daily creativity:** Schedule a time each day, even if just for 10 minutes, to do something creative. There are endless possibilities for this creative time! You can dance to your favorite tunes (don't worry, no one is watching), pick up a paintbrush for the first time since grade school, take pictures of flowers, or try your hand at poetry. You can even incorporate a creativity mantra into your daily meditation (see Chapter 5). Try chanting something like "I live a creative life" as you sit quietly and breath, and allow creative ideas to flood your mind. Repeat this time of creativity daily for at least 3 weeks, even if you are uncertain or feeling a tad embarrassed about doing it. You will probably find that your thoughts about your own creativity will change with the passing weeks.

- **Observe creativity:** Gather inspiration from the creativity of others. Go to art museums, listen to music and attend dance performances. You can even get inspired by the creativity of nature by going for a walk in the woods. Bring your binoculars!

- **Do everyday things in a different way:** When you take your everyday tasks and force yourself to do them differently, you make your brain think more creatively. For a change, try writing with your non-dominant hand or driving to work via a completely new and different route. Exercise in the morning if you usually go to the gym at night or vice versa. Eat breakfast for dinner. Hand-write a letter instead of typing an email. Visit a new place on the weekend, or eat a fruit that you have never tried.

- **Make a creative space:** If you have a whole extra room in your house, use this; otherwise, a corner of a room will work just fine. Set aside this space for any creative endeavors that interest you.

Bring in any tools that you might use for your creating, display anything you have already made, and put up inspiration from other creators that you admire. Try putting up little notes to yourself that remind you that you are creative and you are an artist! It may feel cheesy, but it really works.

- **Give yourself time:** Creativity cannot be forced. If you find that, in spite of your best efforts, the creative juices aren't flowing, just relax and notice your thoughts and feelings. You may find that inspiration hits you at the strangest of times.

- **Rewire your inner critic:** Criticizing your own efforts may have its time and place eventually, but the inner critic has no place in your early efforts. Do not let anxiety or negative self-talk keep you from trying! Remind yourself that all creative artists started from somewhere, and you have the same potential as any of them. It is ok to acknowledge your anxiety and the reasons behind it, but talk back to it and then let it go. Allow yourself to make mistakes, because these are part of the creative process. If you find that inner criticism is still blocking you, incorporate positive affirmations into your meditations (again, see Chapter 5). An example is "I am fine just as I am." When you breathe in, think "I am fine…"; when you breathe out, think "just as I am…" Make your inhales and exhales long, slow and deep, lasting for 5 seconds each if possible.

- **Get moving**: People tend to have more creative ideas after exercise. Physical activity clears the mind, improves mood and raises energy for a significant period of time afterward. Just 20 minutes of aerobic exercise can help free your creative ideas. You may want to bring along a pencil and a little bit of paper, though – you never know when a creative idea may strike you!

- **Stretch your muscles:** After your period of aerobic exercise, be sure to stretch out your muscles. This helps to bring oxygen to your brain and symbolically releases any emotional blocks. Try standing tall and extending your arms behind you. Then stretch your arms to the sides and gently twist your spine to one side, then the other. Gently stretch your neck by lowering your head to one shoulder, then the other. Bend at the waist and reach towards your toes.

- **Bring your creativity with you:** Carry a notebook and pen with you or a handheld recorder. You never know when inspiration may strike you, and you want to be able to record it when it does!

- **Practice mindfulness:** See Chapter 6 for a full description!

- **Ask questions:** You can spark your creative thinking by wondering about things that have previously escaped your attention. How does a water filter work? How many hairs are on your head? At what rate do your fingernails grow? How many gallons of water are in the nearest lake? By questioning things that you don't normally think about, you create new pathways in your brain and open up potential new lines of investigation to pursue.

- **Say "Yes!":** When someone invites you to see an eclectic music group or try a new restaurant, say yes! When someone suggests a group camping trip or taking a dance class, give it a try. It probably won't hurt you…and you will likely come home with some new ideas, or at least an entertaining story or two.

- **Find a creative community:** Many productive artists find inspiration from each other. Find a group with similar interests to your own, such as a knitting group, painting class, choir, writing group, or improv troupe. If you cannot find a group, make one! Try posting invitations at local coffee shops or searching online forums for people with similar creative interests.

- **Imitate:** You've heard that imitation is the most sincere form of flattery. This is true, but it can also be a source of inspiration. Try recreating a favorite artist's work, but not exactly in the same way that they did it. For example, make it smaller or bigger, or transfer it to a different medium. If you love a particular painting, try recreating it with charcoal or colored pencils. Imitate a favorite author's writing style, but use your own words.

Even if some of these suggestions seem a bit far-fetched or out of your comfort zone, that is sort of the whole point. Creative thinking stretches your imagination beyond your norm, whatever that may be. So, go ahead and give them all a try, at least once. You may be surprised at the results. Not only will you find yourself thinking more creatively than you thought possible, but your memory will begin functioning more efficiently with each creative endeavor.

The Reverse Holds True, Too

As it turns out, creativity and memory are so intrinsically linked that the relationship works in reverse. You have just learned how to think creatively in order to inspire your memory. But you will also find that your creative juices start to flow more freely as your memory abilities get sharper and stronger, too.

There is a reason that major creative breakthroughs tend to happen after a person has spent many years in their field. It is because they draw on previous experiences to come up with new ideas. It can take years, or even decades, to absorb the many small pieces of mental material that combine to feed a new insight. Old experiences are the raw material for creativity. As you strengthen your ability to recall memories, you may find that you are more creative than you ever imagined. This reciprocal relationship is both fascinating and exciting. Just imagine the creative possibilities that may open up for you as you flex your memory muscles!

Chapter 9: The Power of Emotional Recall

Of all the processes that go on in our brains, emotions are perhaps the most mysterious. It seems that these things that we call feelings are everywhere, inescapable, and sometimes so powerful that they temporarily incapacitate us. They are both visible and invisible, and they have connections to physical and spiritual sensations. They are the inspiration to many creative endeavors and the downfall of many otherwise powerful individuals. They have the power to ruin an entire week or create the greatest day of your life. But what are they?

What are Emotions?

By simplistic definition, emotions are natural states of mind caused by our circumstances, relationships or mood. But they are so much more than this. They are sensations generated by our brains that can affect our whole being, both physically and spiritually. They are combinations of physical stimuli, thoughts and the urge to act.

When we feel a powerful emotion, our body reacts with physical sensations. Your stomach can feel "jittery" when you are afraid. Your pulse quickens and you sweat when you are nervous or excited.

Emotions are also tied to thoughts. Although sometimes it's difficult to tell which came first, usually a specific thought leads to a specific emotion, although this succession usually happens so rapidly that you cannot separate the two without effort. Once you feel a specific emotion, you usually act on it in some small or large way. When you feel happy, you smile. When you are sad, you may cry or lower your head. When you are angry, you may yell or even fight.

Emotions cause us to act in specific ways and say specific things, often without even meaning to. How many times have you said or done something in the heat of the moment, and then later regretted your emotional course of action? But the way you were feeling at the time was so powerful that you felt you had no choice but to act as you did.

Emotions and Memory

Since emotions are so closely tied to our words, actions and physical sensations, it makes sense that they have a very close relationship with memories. In fact, we are typically much more likely to remember a specific person, place, thing or event if it is tied with a powerful emotion or two. For example, you may have very little recollection of your math teacher in ninth grade because nothing particularly exciting ever happened in that class. However, during that same year, you may have had a History teacher who was always full of jokes and fascinating stories. He made you laugh and inspired you by his manner of teaching. Your feelings of humor, delight, and hope from your experiences with that particular teacher make him stand out in your memories.

In fact, recent research suggests that emotions, not personal significance, make certain experiences stand out in our memories. Sometimes emotions even warp our memories and make them inaccurate. If you are given instructions for a task, but then something happens that causes strong emotions, you may not be able to recall the instructions.

We also tend to treat memories differently depending on the emotions associated with them. If a memory is associated with unpleasant emotions, we might go to great lengths to avoid that memory. We may even go so far as to unconsciously block those memories, potentially to the point that we don't remember them at all. Sometimes extremely unpleasant memories, both conscious and unconscious, can be the root of serious psychological issues.

On the other hand, we like to retell the story of particularly happy or triumphant memories so that we can relive those more desirable emotions. We might remember the "happiest day of our life" in great detail, even down to exactly what we were wearing on that day.

Our emotions also affect our ability to recall past events. For example, when you are depressed, you are more likely to remember negative experiences. When you are experiencing an emotional "high," you recall other times when you have felt the same elevated mood. In other words, your mood when you *retrieve* a memory often matches the mood you were in when that memory was first *encoded* (see Chapter 1 for more about encoding and retrieval).

Using Emotions to Improve Memory Ability

When you simply allow emotions to affect physical reaction and your ability to recall experiences, you are ruled by your emotions. You give your feelings the power to keep you from remembering certain things and block important details. But by learning to *transform your emotional habits*, you can improve your overall recall ability for both past and future experiences. The idea is to be in touch with your emotions and accept them without letting them master you.

By practicing acceptance of your whole range of emotions, you will still be able to feel them but they will not be able to cloud your recall ability. An additional side benefit is that you will become less reactive to your emotions. You will have the power of choice over how you behave in situations, rather than your emotions telling you how to act and react.

Over the next several weeks, try each of the following suggestions to gradually transform your emotional habits and learn acceptance of your feelings:

- **Identify emotional triggers:** When you know that certain circumstances can cause specific emotions in you, you can be prepared for these feelings in advance even if you have no control over the triggers. In other words, forewarned is forearmed. Physical triggers can include other people's expressions or body postures, certain foods or beverages, medications, hormonal fluctuations, and illness. Mental triggers are things like religious beliefs of yourself and others, attitudes, comparisons to others, and making decisions. Environmental triggers can be certain types of weather, being in crowded places, or being isolated.

Take some time to identify your emotional triggers. If there are any you can eliminate (like certain foods), get rid of them! Unfortunately, there is no way to get rid of the majority of our emotional triggers. But if you know in advance that you get anxious in crowds or nervous when you have to make a decision, you can prepare yourself for this in advance. Once you know what to expect, your emotions may not seem so bad. You'll find that you are able to experience them and know that they will come to an end once the trigger has passed.

- **Notice your inner talk:** The way that you speak to yourself can have a great impact on your emotions. When you are feeling worthless and depressed, it may be because you are telling yourself that you are worthless. Take a moment to ask yourself why you are feeling a certain way and what you have been telling yourself to fuel that emotion. Try reframing your inner talk in a more gentle and positive manner. Talk to yourself as you would a dear friend or a beloved child. Chances are that you are much harsher with yourself than you would be with anyone else, and you don't deserve that negativity! This change of inner talk can take a lot of practice, but do not give up.

- **Reframe problems**: Often, our emotions are caused by our perspective of a particular problem. For example, you may feel down because you made a mistake or you are experiencing a conflict with someone. Instead of being afraid, sad or anxious about this problem, try viewing it as an opportunity for growth and learning. Like changing your negative inner talk, this can take a lot of practice, because you are working to change years of a specific way of thinking and feeling. Be persistent, and you'll find that you become more optimistic about problems than you ever thought possible!

- **Sit with your emotions:** This is a particular form of mindfulness (further discussed in Chapter 6) that can be tremendously beneficial to transforming your emotional habits. When you are feeling a certain way (especially when you want to act on a strong emotion), take a moment to name it, either out loud or in your head. Then pause and focus on your breath as it goes in and out of your body, instead of acting. Next, get in touch with your physical sensations. Start by noticing your feet on the ground, or your seat and back on a chair. Then become aware of your heartbeat and any sensations in your stomach, chest, and throat. Keep breathing slowly in and out. Notice where you feel the emotion most strongly in your body and how it feels. Perhaps it is a prickly sensation in the back of your neck or a tightness in your chest. Maybe you associate certain sounds or smells with it.

As you explore the sensations with your emotion, resist the urge to act on them. Visualize moving the emotion into the area around your heart and pay attention to how it shifts. It may feel sharper at first, and then soften. Notice your perspective shifting.

Keep practicing this emotional awareness each time a strong emotion overtakes you. In time, you will find a new understanding of your emotions and the ability to regulate your response to them.

- **Express your emotions:** Although the idea is to not react to emotions, it is essential to still express them. Stifling strong feelings is dangerous to your physical and psychological well-being, so you must find appropriate ways to let them out. When you are angry, a brisk walk may help or you may need to scream into a pillow, or even pound on the pillow. When you are sad, you may benefit from a cleansing cry alone or on a friend's shoulder. If you find that you regularly experience anger or frustration, perhaps you should try enrolling in an exercise class or sports team. Physical activity is a great way of channeling strong emotions in an appropriate way. If you are grieving, journal about it, seek solace from a pet or a friend and give yourself time to work through the grief. One exception to emotional expression can be fear, so keep reading to learn how to handle feelings of fear.

- **Learn to tone down fear:** Repeated expressions of fear or reactions to things that strike fear in your heart can lead to phobias or panic attacks. Fear can take on a life of its own and gain the power to control all aspects of your life. When you are feeling fearful (unless you are actually in a dangerous situation; then, by all means, get away from it!), pause to notice the facts of the situation. What is happening in this exact moment? Notice your self-talk and tone down the fear from a catastrophic level to an approachable problem. Instead of picturing the worst possible outcome, picture yourself solving the problem and conquering your fear. Remind yourself that you have only been imagining one possible future, not the only one. Then imagine a new, more positive outcome.

- **Let emotional intensity fade:** When you are feeling strong emotions, take a timeout before acting. This "time out" could be any duration from a few minutes to a few days, depending on the situation. Give yourself appropriate healthy distractions, like exercise or creative outlets (see Chapter 8). Then revisit the problem or situation that is causing your emotions and see how you feel about it.

- **Try on opposite emotions**: If you are feeling a certain way that makes you uncomfortable, try challenging yourself to feel differently. If you are angry at someone, work to find things about them that you are grateful for. If you are envious of someone else's success, try being happy for them and celebrating their good fortune. These efforts will help you balance your emotions and ward off the tendency for resentment.

- **Laugh:** During particularly tense, frustrating or upsetting times, take a break to find some comedy. Look up stupid jokes or comedy sketches online. Even fake laughter has been known to help change your mood.

Emotions can be great teachers, once we learn to accept and even embrace them. Awareness of your emotions can teach you valuable lessons about yourself, like how you make choices, who your best friends are, and what your priorities are. Once you have learned to recognize and accept your emotions, you'll find that, with practice, you will have better ability to recall things that happen, no matter how you were feeling at the time.

Chapter 10: Small Tips and Tricks for Training Your Memory

So far, we have covered all of the health when it comes to better memory. We have covered your physical health, including diet, exercise, and sleep. We have also covered your psychological and spiritual health by teaching you how to meditate, be mindful, train your creativity and practice awareness and acceptance of your emotions. Each of these processes is a piece of the puzzle that lead to better brain health and stronger memory abilities. But we still have a few tricks up our sleeves.

You may be looking for helpful hints for studying for your next test or memorizing a speech for the next corporate banquet. Or perhaps you have started incorporating all of the healthy suggestions in the previous chapter and you are ready to impress your friends by becoming a true memory master. You will find the tips and techniques that you desire in these final two chapters. This chapter outlines easy ways to quickly memorize information, and the next chapter covers some major techniques for overhauling your memory powers.

No matter what you are trying to learn and remember, there are quite a few tricks that the memory experts swear by for better recall. Try the following ideas as you learn the key points of a presentation or study for an exam:

- **Take in information slowly**: It is pretty tempting to procrastinate on your studies and then "cram" for an exam, or to read as much of your textbook as possible so you can relax for the rest of the week. But you will find that memorization is more effective if you slow the pace of learning and take in the information over several days or even weeks. If you have an exam on ten chapters in a week, try studying two chapters per night, and then reviewing for a couple of days. If you are a teacher who needs to memorize the names of your students, learn four or five names per day and you should have the whole class memorized in a week or two.

- **Repetition is key**: You can hardly expect to memorize a large chunk of material in a few days, and then recall it again in a month without reviewing it in between. For long-term recall, you must repeat! Remember, new information represents a new pathway in your brain. If you want to remember the information and commit it to your long-term memory, you have to travel that pathway frequently! The more you review, the stronger the neural pathway gets. For example, if you are learning how to conjugate German verbs, set aside time to practice and recite the conjugations at least every other day for a couple weeks, then once every few days, then once a week.

- **Mnemonic devices:** A mnemonic device is any learning technique that helps you remember information. A classic example of this is the phrase "My Very Excellent Mother Just Served Us Nine Pizzas" for remembering the order of the nine planets. Or there is the rhyme for the months that helps you remember which of them have 31 days and which have 30 days. Or perhaps you have learned the method of keeping track of the month lengths by counting them on your knuckles. When it comes to these little memory tricks, the possibilities are endless as long as it helps you. If it is a list of things in a specific order, try coming up with a clever phrase, like the planet illustration. Or come up with a rhyme, song or image to help you remember.

- **Picture associations (visualization)**: A picture association or visualization is an image that you conjure in your brain by converting words to the nearest sounding word or words that you can think of. These are especially helpful when it comes to efforts to remember people's names. Someone named Shelly Baker could be visualized as wearing a baker's hat and apron, with pictures of shells on the apron. For someone named Ben, you can picture Big Ben in London, with Ben's face in place of the clock. For someone named Vincent, picture the famous self-portrait of the painter, van Gogh, only with Vincent's face in place of the painter's face. For someone named Sandy, imagine that person on a beach. The picture does not have to be anything special, just something that helps you remember.

- **Chewing gum:** It sounds a little silly, you may experience improved memory abilities if you try chewing some gum while you are learning some new information. This may not work, because only limited research has been done on the concept, but it is worth a try. One study suggested that participants had more accurate memory recall and better reaction times if they chewed gum. It has been speculated that chewing gum may increase activity in the hippocampus, which is involved in memory encoding and retrieval. Even if it may not work, it is certainly worth a try!

- **Mind mapping:** Mind mapping is a different way of visualizing information to make memorization easier. In this technique, you visually organize information in a way that makes it simpler to break into categories and remember systematically. The basic idea is to draw a diagram that shows relationships and the hierarchal organization of pieces of a whole. You draw a diagram, with the main idea at the center, and branches leading to sub-topics all around the main idea. The sub-topics can have more branches, or lists of simple details, drawn around them. An easy way to get good examples of this is to Google "mind map." You may find that you memorize information better by incorporating different colors into your mind map or writing in small and large letters to emphasize the importance of ideas.

- **"Chunking" information:** This idea correlates with taking in information slowly. Not only should you slow the rate at which you consume new material, but it helps to break it up into smaller, "bite-sized" pieces. If you are want to memorize an extremely long number, like the first 100 digits of pi, try breaking it into sequences of 10 numbers and memorizing the short sequences once at a time, like individual phone numbers. Other situations in which this technique might be helpful are memorizing speeches for weddings or monologues for a play.

All of the above techniques make use of the way that your memory already works, which is by associating old information with new information. In other words, when you take the familiar link it to something unfamiliar, the new and unfamiliar can become unforgettable. Each of them is tried and true, and the best part is that none of them require much time to help you. But if you're looking to memorize even more information, or continue to enhance your memory abilities to astonishing levels, read on to the next chapter.

Chapter 11: Becoming a Memory Champion

If you're not satisfied with boosting your brain health and learning various tips and tricks for various overall learning, this is the chapter you have been waiting for. This final chapter includes the techniques that those with the so-called "photographic memories" used to obtain memory greatness. These techniques are used by people who win memory championships and by those are employed by the military as spies. These are the people whose lives, or at least reputations, depend on having a superb memory. By using these techniques, you can reach the level of memory greatness that you have dreamed about!

The Military Method

Disclaimer: Although this method is touted as the "military method," there is no actual proof that this method is used by the military to train their operatives. However, it is suggested as a way of enhancing your ability to quickly memorize large amounts of information, and it has been touted by many as an effective method of training your memory. It does not take much time out of each day, so it is certainly worth a try!

The materials you will need for this method of memory training are a small bright lamp and a piece of darkly colored paper. You also need the written or typed book or document that you are planning to memorize.

Follow these steps:

1. Commit to approximately 15 minutes per day to practice.

2. Designate a quiet place in your house where you can practice. It is important that you are able to make the room dark, so use a closet if necessary. Bring your desk lamp in that area.

3. In your dark colored piece of paper, cut out a rectangle-shaped hole that is about the size of a paragraph on your document or book.

4. Put the paper on top of your document or book. Make sure that the paragraph you want to memorize first shows through the hole that you cut in the paper.

5. Place your document or book just far enough from your eyes to be able to see it easily and quickly.

6. Turn all of the lights off, and make sure the room is completely dark. Allow your eyes time to adjust to the darkness, so that you can begin to make out shapes in the darkness.

7. While looking at the place where your book or document is, turn on the small light for less than a second and then turn it off.

8. During that brief moment, your eyes will have taken a mental picture of the paragraph that shows through the hole

in your dark piece of paper. Focus on that image in your brain. When it has faded from your mind's eye completely, turn the lamp back on for another fraction of a second and then it off again. Always keep looking at the paragraph you are trying to memorize.

9. Do this repeatedly, for about 15 minutes every day, until you have the entire paragraph memorized without any errors whatsoever. Do not skip any days; according to some sources, skipping a day can set you back by an entire week.

10. If you use this technique, combined with all that you have already learned in this guide and the rest of the techniques described in this chapter, you will find that your memory is as close to

"photographic" as you could ever imagine.

The Memory Palace

This method is a very powerful memory technique that has been proven to be effective, easy to learn, and a little fun to boot. It employs the method of visualization that you learned in the last chapter, but on a more complex level. Simply follow these steps to use this technique, and you will find it can be helpful in many situations:

1. **Choose a palace**. Although it is called a palace, it does not have to be a literal palace. Simply visualize a place with which you are extremely familiar. This can be your own home or school, for example. The key is to pick a place that you can easily picture in great detail. Also, try to visualize a specific walking route within your palace instead of just

seeing it as a scene. So, if your palace is your home, picture a specific order of walking through it, room by room. Other places that you could choose might be the place where you work, a local park or pathway that you walk or jog regularly, or familiar streets in your neighborhood.

2. **List Memorable and Important Features:** As you mentally tour your chosen palace, pay attention to the distinctive features in it. For example, if you chose your place of employ, the first feature might be the parking lot. Now walk your chosen pathway through your palace, taking note of each room or destination in the order that you have chosen. The more detail you notice, the better. Perhaps you scan each room from right to left, noticing features in order as you scan. Keep making mental

notes of each feature as you go. Each feature that you notice will be a memory "slot" that you use later as you memorize pieces of information.

3. **Fully Imprint Your Palace in Your Mind:** Go through your memory palace over and over, making note of the same features each time until you have it fully memorized. This is important! If you do not have it completely and reliably memorized, the technique will not work for you. If necessary, write down each detail of your palace or draw a picture of it. Repeat your route through your palace aloud if that helps. Remember to always look at your chosen features of the palace in the same order and from the same perspective. Even when you think you have it fully memorized, go over it a few more times. You need to be confident in your knowledge of the

palace and it is impossible to "overlearn" your mental path through it.

4. **Start using your palace:** Try using your palace to memorize something simple at first, like a grocery list. Start by visualizing the first thing on the list in association with the first feature of your palace. If the first feature of your palace is the parking lot and the first thing on your grocery list is eggs, picture eggs all over the parking lot. Picture little egg cars parked in the parking spots, smashed eggs all over the blacktop, and adorable winged eggs chirping happily in the trees. Got it? Next, let's say that the second feature of your memory palace is the front door of your office building and the second item on your grocery list is a carton of milk. Try picturing the front door as a milk carton, with lots of cold milk running

out from under the door, forming little pools of milk around the entrance.

Continue this visualization until you have placed each item on your grocery list firmly in association with a feature of your memory palace.

5. **Re-visit your palace:** Now that you have finished placing all of the items on your list, do some rehearsal. Repeat the journey once or twice so that you are sure you know the order of your list and you have not left anything out. If you have been successful at always starting at the same point and following the same route, your memorized list will come to your mind quickly as you visualize the pathway through your palace.

6. **Keep using your palace** to memorize longer lists and more intricate sets of information. You'll be amazed at how much you can remember with this technique!

Peg System

This is another, somewhat simpler method of memorizing lists of information. It is simpler than the memory palace, but you may not be able to remember as much information with this one. The way it works is by pre-memorizing a simple list of words that are associated with numbers. The words that you memorize are the "pegs" in the system. It is generally useful to make the words rhyme with the numbers, or associate them with a well-known list, like the names of the seven books of the Harry Potter series.

For example:

One = sun

Two = glue

Three = key

Four = store

Five = drive

Six = bricks

Seven = Kevin

Eight = crate

Nine = line

Ten = pen

Next, when you need to remember a list of items, try associating each item from your list to the corresponding number peg. For example, we'll try another shopping list. If the first item on the list is bacon, picture a sun with bacon sizzling on its surface. If the second item is bread, picture a loaf of bread with all of the pieces stuck together with glue. Get the idea? If your list is longer than your peg system, you can repeat it in groupings of ten (or seven, if you are using Harry Potter books). This

method is simple but generally very effective. If you are memorizing vast quantities of information, we suggest returning to the memory palace described above.

The Deck of Cards Memorization Method

Believe it or not, there are memory masters who can easily memorize the order of a randomly shuffled deck of 52 cards in less than two minutes! This feat is required in order to become a Grand Master of Memory at an official World Memory Championship (this is a real event).

One of these impressive card deck memorizers is Nelson Dellis, a four-time winner of the USA Memory Championship. When asked for a technique on how to memorize a shuffled deck of cards, he outlined the following steps:

1. **Start with face cards.** Separate the face cards from the deck. There should be twelve of them: Jack, Queen, and King from all four suits. You'll start by just memorizing the order of these twelve, then increase to half a deck, then

a whole deck. In this way, you set small, realistic goals to accomplish your overall goal. Small victories will keep you going as you see your abilities improve.

2. **Person/Action/Object (a.k.a. PAO)** This step uses the technique of "chunking" information that you learned in the previous chapter. By taking 52 cards and dividing them into groups of 3, you reduce your list of 52 down to a manageable 17 (with one extra at the end). Person/Action/Object also takes advantage of the visualization technique previously discussed in Chapter 10. We'll start with the 12 face cards that you set aside before.

   a. Associate a person with each of the 12 face cards. It doesn't matter who the card reminds you of as long as it is easy to remember. Dellis says that the King of Clubs reminds him of Tiger Woods, because of golf clubs. King of Hearts reminds him of his dad, and King of diamonds reminds him of Donald Trump.

b. Then decide on an action and an object for each person. For example, the King of Clubs is Tiger Woods, he plays golf, and his object is obviously a golf club.

c. Once you have the idea of PAO (Person/Action/Object) for each card, you can group the cards into sets of 3. The first card will be the assigned Person, the second is its Action, and the third is an Object. This turns a group of three cards into just one image. For example, the three cards might be the King of Clubs, followed by the King of Hearts, followed by the King of Diamonds. You would picture Tiger Woods, doing heart surgery (the action), on a casino (the object).

3. **Use Your Memory Palace.** If things did not seem tricky before, they are about to. Here you use the memory palace technique you learned earlier in this chapter because you need a place to store each of the groups of cards as you memorize them. If your palace is your home and the first feature of your home is the lawn, you would picture Tiger Woods on your lawn, operating on a heart, on a casino.

4. **Expand to half a deck, then the whole deck.** Once you have been able to memorize the face cards, the next step is for you to figure out PAOs for each card in the rest of the deck. This can be tricky, so use your imagination. You can start by seeing if any of them are obvious to you. Assign significant cards to your friends, family and beloved pets first. Be sure to give each one a person, an action, and an object. For example, the 3 of Hearts could be your three-legged cat. The action could be eating, and the object could be cat kibble.

For the less obvious cards, the master memorizer Dellis suggests using something called the Dominic System, which is a code for numbers and suits that translates into letters, which then represents the initials of a person or character. We'll work through an example so you can grasp it.

The system:

The first 8 numbers are represented by the letters A through H, then the number 9 is represented by the letter N and the number 0 is represented by the letter O.

For the suits, Clubs = C; Diamonds = D; Spades = S; Hearts = H.

For example, Ace of Spades is an A and an S. Ace = A, Spades = S.

A.S. = Arnold Schwarzenegger/weightlifting/barbell.

5 of Clubs is E and C.

E.C. = Eric Clapton/playing guitar/guitar.

2 of Diamonds is B and D.

B.D. = Bo Derek (an actress, from the movie *Tommy Boy*)/braiding/hair.

So if you had the three cards together, in order, you would have Arnold Schwarzenegger, playing guitar on his hair.

You would place this rather odd image wherever it belongs in your memory palace so you know the order that you found it in the deck. This system is flexible and easy to personalize so that you can assign significance to cards as you see fit and as you will best be able to remember them.

5. **Practice!** After you put together all 17 sets of 3 (plus one extra), you may be able to memorize an entire deck at your first try. To gain speed, all you need to do is practice, practice, practice! If you practice each day, you'll gradually cut your speed impressively as you gain the ability to recognize your assigned images and PAO for each card and gain confidence.

Seriously, Just Keep Practicing

With all of the techniques above and any amount of information that you wish to memorize, the key is "practice makes perfect."

There's certainly no shame in sticking to the first 9 or 10 chapters of this book and using the tips to become the healthiest and sharpest version of yourself. Your memory abilities will be as strong as ever, and they will just keep improving as you eat healthier, exercise, get plenty of sleep and practice your meditation, creativity and emotional mindfulness.

However, for those who have lofty ambitions of conquering great feats of memory, it's time to embrace the techniques outlined in the last part of this guide. You'll find that with enough dedication and determination, you'll be impressing everyone with your memory prowess. Who knows, there could be a national or worldwide memory championship in your near future!

Conclusion

Thanks for making it through to the end of *Photographic Memory: 10 Steps to Remember Anything Superfast*. Let's hope it was informative and able to provide you with all of the tools you need to achieve your goals whatever they may be.

The next step is to put all that you have learned to good use! This is not the type of book that you can read and just put away if you want it to transform your life. Keep if available as a reference so you can use it as often as necessary. Keep trying the tips for nutrition, exercise, and sleep until you have found a good and healthy balance for your brain. Incorporate the meditation and mindfulness practices into your daily routines to maximize your awareness and further enhance your memory abilities. Don't forget to keep a busy and meaningful social calendar, especially if you are retired! Staying active is the key to retaining a youthful memory.

Next, keep trying different methods of creativity from Chapter 8. Find your own creative niche and prepare to be amazed as your creative endeavors enhance the power of your memory. Spend some time and effort in creating emotional awareness within you so that you can learn to appreciate your feelings but not allow them to interfere with your ability to recall experiences.

When you face an everyday memorization task, refer to Chapter 10 for help! With a little practice, you will find that you are able to remember your shopping lists, Christmas lists and daily appointments without writing them down. Finally, if you have goals of competing in memory challenges or you just want to see how far your own memory can take you, make Chapter 11 your bible. Find time in each day to practice the techniques described, and before long, your friends will be describing you as the one with the "photographic memory!" Don't worry, your secret is safe with us!

www.ingramcontent.com/pod-product-compliance
Lightning Source LLC
Chambersburg PA
CBHW071351080526
44587CB00017B/3060